The Instant Answer Book of
COUNTRIES

Annabel Warrender and Jenny Tyler

Illustrated by Joseph McEwan
and Graham Round

Designed by Graham Round

Australia

India

Canada

West Germany

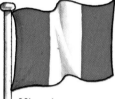
Nigeria

China

Saudi Arabia

France

Greece

Sweden

New Zealand

Turkey

Denmark

Italy

U.S.A.

Spain

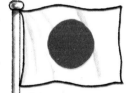
Japan

U.S.S.R.

Netherlands

Brazil

Contents

First published in 1978 by Usborne Publishing Ltd, 20 Garrick Street, London WC2E 9BJ, England. Reprinted in 1979.
Copyright © 1978 Usborne Publishing Ltd.
Published in the U.S.A. by Hayes Books, 4235 South Memorial Drive, Tulsa, Oklahoma, U.S.A.
Published in Canada by Hayes Publishing Ltd, Burlington, Ontario.
Printed by Waterlow (Dunstable) Ltd, England.

Countries and populations

The world is divided up into areas called countries. No two countries are alike; some are bigger than others, some have more people living in them. Some are rich and powerful and others are very poor. Most of the countries in the world today are independent, which means that they rule themselves.

What is a country?

Each independent country has its own government which decides how the country should be run. Its laws must be obeyed by everyone who lives or visits there.

Countries are separated from each other by borders or frontiers, which are decided by international agreements. Some countries' borders are still being disputed.

Every country has its own flag with special colours and design on it.

Most countries have a traditional national costume.

Most countries have a special song called their national anthem.

How many countries are there?

In 1900 there were 53 independent countries. Today there are 161. There are still 62 other areas, called territories, which are ruled by other countries.

Did you know?

The U.S.S.R. is 50 million times bigger than the Vatican City. If the U.S.S.R. were the size of a football pitch, then the Vatican City would be a ¼ the size of a postage stamp.

These are the ten countries with the largest areas.

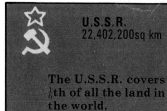
U.S.S.R. 22,402,200sq km

The U.S.S.R. covers ⅙th of all the land in the world.

CANADA 9,976,139 sq km

CHINA 9,596,961 sq km

U.S.A. 9,363,123 sq km

BRAZIL 8,511,965 sq km

AUSTRALIA 7,686,848sq km

INDIA 3,287,590sq km

ARGENTINA 2,776,898sq km

SUDAN 2,505,800sq km

ALGERIA 2,381,741sq km

Which are the smallest countries?

1 THE VATICAN CITY 0.4sq km

2 MONACO 2sq km

3  SAN MARINO 61sq km

4 LIECHTENSTEIN 160sq km

5 MALTA 316sq km

6  SEYCHELLES 376sq km

7 BARBADOS 431sq km

8 ANDORRA 453sq km

9 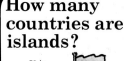 SINGAPORE 531sq km

Which is the oldest country?

Iran, or Persia as it was called until 1934, has been independent since 529 BC. It is the oldest country in the world.

Which is the newest country?

The Solomon Islands became independent from Great Britain on 7 July 1978.

How many countries are islands?

32 of the independent countries in the world are islands.

How many countries have no sea coast?

There are 26 countries which have no coastline at all.

How many people are in the world?

The number of people in the world is growing by $1\frac{1}{2}$ million every week. There are about 4,200 million people in the world at the moment, but if the world's population keeps on growing at this rate, there will be twice this number in only 35 years time.

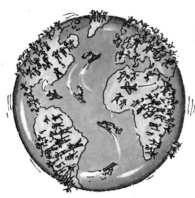

Peoples' ages

	Under 15	Between 15 and 64	Over 64
WORLD	36%	58%	6%
AFRICA	40%	57%	3%
EUROPE	24%	64%	12%

Which countries have the most people?

These countries have most people though they are not the most crowded

CHINA 860 million people

INDIA 610 million people

U.S.S.R. 257 million people

U.S.A. 215 million people

Which countries have least people?

These four countries have the smallest populations in the world.

VATICAN CITY 1,000 people

NAURU 7,300 people

SAN MARINO 20,000 people

MONACO 30,000 people

The most crowded countries

The most crowded areas of the world are Europe and Asia. The three most crowded countries in the world are:

MONACO 16,938 people per sq km

SINGAPORE 3,872 people per sq km

VATICAN CITY 1,645 people per sq km

The emptiest countries

Some parts of the world are too cold, too hot, too dry, or too mountainous for people to live in. Some countries have large areas where almost no-one lives at all. These are the least crowded countries.

1 person per sq km

LIBYA MAURITANIA MONGOLIA BOTSWANA

2 people per sq km

AUSTRALIA CANADA GABON ICELAND

3 people per sq km

CHAD OMAN SURINAM

Where are there more women?

There are more women than men in the U.S.S.R. For every 100 women, there are only 85 men.

Did you know?

If all the people in China stood on each other's shoulders, they would make three chains stretching from the Earth to the Moon.

Which country's population is growing the fastest?

If the population of Kuwait continues to grow as fast as it is at the moment, it will double in $11\frac{1}{2}$ years.

Populations that are getting smaller

The population of Malta is decreasing at the moment. If it continues to do so at the same rate, in 40 years time the population would be half what it is today.

Rich and poor countries

The world's wealth is very unevenly shared out. Four countries, which together have only 15% of the world's people, own 50% of the world's wealth.

In the rich countries most people work in factories, making manufactured goods. Some countries are rich because they have valuable raw materials, such as oil, which they sell to other countries. In the poor countries, most people work on the land, growing food for themselves to eat.

Did you know?

Hong Kong has the lowest value notes in the world—its one cent notes are worth about $\frac{1}{12}$ penny.

Which are the richest countries?

The richest countries are those which produce and sell the most goods, raw materials and services (such as banking and transport).

U.S.A. £595,273 million a year

U.S.S.R. £238,340 million a year

JAPAN £192,505 million a year

W. GERMANY £163,734 million a year

Most exports

Countries which produce more goods than they need, sell or export them to other countries. These countries export the most.

U.S.A. £42,872 million worth of goods a year

W. GERMANY £37,795 million worth of goods a year

JAPAN £23,692 million worth of goods a year

FRANCE £19,751 million worth of goods a year

The steel industry

These countries produce the most steel:

U.S.S.R. 141 million tonnes a year

U.S.A. 106 million tonnes a year

JAPAN 102 million tonnes a year

W. GERMANY 40 million tonnes a year

Together the U.S.S.R., Japan, the U.S.A. and West Germany own over half of the world's wealth.

Oil-rich countries

Middle East countries have great quantities of oil in their land. They have recently become very rich through selling this oil. About 40% of the world's oil comes from Middle East countries.

How rich are people in different parts of the world?

To find out how rich people are, we have taken all the wealth produced in a year by a country and divided it evenly among the people who live there. These eight countries have been chosen to show the great differences in wealth around the world.

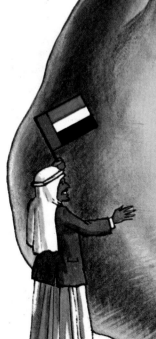

UNITED ARAB EMIRATES £6,813 a year

U.S.A. £2,530 a year

AUSTRALIA £2,325 a year

How high is the standard of living in different countries?

The type of house you live in, the sort of food you eat, and the kinds of things you own all make up your "standard of living". In the poorer countries most people have a very low standard of living, with scarcely enough to eat. Many people live in houses with no running water or electricity. These pictures show some of the differences in living standards between poor and rich countries.

How many people have running water in their houses?

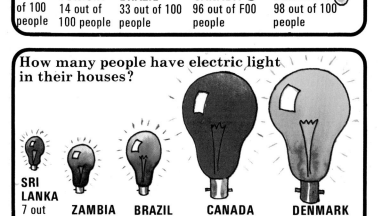

SRI LANKA 4 out of 100 people

TUNISIA 14 out of 100 people

BRAZIL 33 out of 100 people

CANADA 96 out of F00 people

DENMARK 98 out of 100 people

How many people have electric light in their houses?

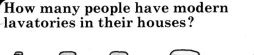

SRI LANKA 7 out of 100 people

ZAMBIA 16 out of 100 people

BRAZIL 53 out of 100 people

CANADA 94 out of 100 people

DENMARK 96 out of 100 people

How many people have modern lavatories in their houses?

SRI LANKA 9 out of 100 people

ALGERIA 34 out of 100 people

BRAZIL 53 out of 100 people

HUNGARY 94 out of 100 people

AUSTRALIA 98 out of 100 people

How many people can read and write?

Here you can see how many adults can read and write in some rich and poor countries:

FRANCE 99 out of 100 adults can read and write.

JAPAN 90 out of 100 adults can read and write.

INDIA 29 out of 100 adults can read and write.

SUDAN 19 out of 100 adults can read and write.

How many doctors are there?

The rich countries have much more money to spend on hospitals and doctors. Here you can see how many doctors there are per person in some rich and poor countries.

WEST GERMANY 516 people per doctor

AUSTRALIA 721 people per doctor

INDIA 4,162 people per doctor

CHAD 44,382 people per doctor

Which countries have the most universities?

1 U.S.A. 2,606

2 JAPAN 142

3 U.S.S.R. 121

4 INDIA 88

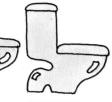

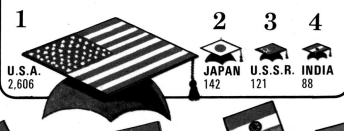

FRANCE £1,910 a year

GHANA £144 a year

CHINA £85 a year

INDIA £53 a year

BHUTAN £25 a year

Precious things

Metals and fuels are some of the most precious things in the world today. We need them to make almost everything we use. Some metals and gemstones are precious because they are so rare. Metals are obtained from minerals which are dug out of the ground. Most fuels are also found in the rocks. They are a very important source of wealth to the countries in which they are found.

Platinum
Found in Canada, South Africa, and the U.S.S.R. Once used to make fake gold, but today is twice as valuable as gold.

Silver
Found in U.S.S.R. Canada, Mexico, and Peru. Over half is used to make photographic chemicals and mirrors.

Rubies
Red gems found in Brazil, Burma, Thailand, Sri Lanka. So rare today, they are more valuable than diamonds.

Sapphires
Found in Australia, Burma, Brazil, Sri Lanka. Come from same mineral—called corundum—as rubies, but are blue instead of red.

Emeralds
Found in Norway, Australia, Colombia. Usually green in colour. Once thought to be magical, and to help women in childbirth.

Gold
South Africa mines 13 times more than any other country. Unlike other metals, gold is found as lumps of metal in the ground.

Where is the deepest mine?

The deepest mine in the world is the Western Deep gold mine in South Africa. It is 3,840 m deep, and could hold 8 Empire State Buildings, one on top of the other.

Where do metals come from?

Minerals which contain metal are called ores. These must be heated to obtain the metal.

Here are some important metals and the countries which mine the most.

IRON (in millions of tonnes of ore a year)

U.S.S.R. 127.5	AUSTRALIA 60.9	U.S.A. 48.8	BRAZIL 46.6

COPPER (in millions of tonnes of metal a year)

U.S.A. 1.5	CHILE 1.0	ZAMBIA 0.8	CANADA 0.7

ALUMINIUM (in millions of tonnes of ore a year)

AUSTRALIA 21.3	GUINEA 10.5	JAMAICA 10.4	SURINAM 4.3

TIN (in millions of tonnes of metal a year)

MALAYSIA 66	U.S.S.R. 30	BOLIVIA 27	INDONESIA 24

GOLD (in tonnes of metal a year)

SOUTH AFRICA 709	CANADA 53	U.S.A. 32	AUSTRALIA

Largest diamond

The largest uncut diamond was the Cullinan, found in South Africa in 1905. It was as big as a man's fist. After cutting it successfully, the Dutch diamond cutter is said to have fainted with relief.

Largest sapphire

The largest sapphire ever found was the Black Star, discovered in Australia. A bust of the late President Eisenhower of the U.S.A. was carved out of it, and given to him.

Did you know?

Coal, graphite (pencil lead) and diamonds are all made of carbon. A diamond will burn, like coal.

When was metal discovered?

Stone Age people carved hammers and knives out of copper ore in about 8000BC. The Egyptians, 4,000 years later, were the first to separate metal from the ore. This picture shows some early Egyptian metal-workers.

Fuel producers

All the world's factories, vehicles and machines need fuel to make them work. Over 90% of the fuels we use are "fossil fuels"—coal, oil and gas—which are found in the ground.

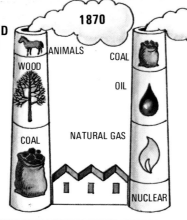

FUELS USED 100 YEARS AGO AND TODAY

1870
ANIMALS
WOOD
COAL

1970
COAL
OIL
NATURAL GAS
NUCLEAR

What are fossil fuels?

Fossil fuels take many hundreds of millions of years to form. They are made up of compressed layers of decayed plants and animals.

How long will it last?

Experts have estimated that by the year 2100 there could be no more oil, coal or gas left in the world, as we are using them up much faster than they are being made.

The top coal-mining countries are:

1 U.S.S.R.
645 million tonnes a year

2 U.S.A.
586 million tonnes a year

3 CHINA
470 million tonnes a year

4 W. GERMANY
220 million tonnes a year

About 6 million tonnes of coal are needed to provide London with electricity for a year.

Most natural gas comes from:

1 U.S.A. 563,000 million cubic metres a year

2 U.S.S.R. 317,000 million cubic metres a year

3 NETHERLANDS 98,000 million cubic metres a year

4 CANADA 88,000 million cubic metres a year

Enough natural gas is produced every second in the U.S.A. to centrally heat over 400 homes for a year.

These are the top oil-producing countries:

1 U.S.S.R.
515 million tonnes a year

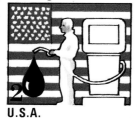

2 U.S.A.
461 million tonnes a year

3 SAUDI ARABIA
422 million tonnes a year

4 IRAN
295 million tonnes a year

You could drive a car to the sun and back 126 times on the oil produced by the U.S.S.R. in a day.

The world's oil producers and users

Countries which have a lot of industry use huge amounts of oil, but usually cannot produce enough for their own needs. Here you can see the difference between the amount of oil used and produced in a year in different parts of the world.

OIL PRODUCED   OIL USED

U.S.S.R.
515 million tonnes — 380 million tonnes

U.S.A.
461 million tonnes — 822 million tonnes

SOUTH AMERICA
233 million tonnes — 187 million tonnes

MIDDLE EAST
1,100 million tonnes — 73 million tonnes

WESTERN EUROPE
45 million tonnes — 706 million tonnes

JAPAN
1 million tonnes — 254 million tonnes

Nuclear fuel

One tonne of the nuclear fuel, uranium, can produce as much energy as 30,000 tonnes of coal.

Top producers of uranium are: Canada, U.S.A., South Africa and France.

Did you know?

About a sixth of the world's oil is not used for fuel, but to make things such as these:

LIPSTICK
CANDLES
NYLON
POLISH
PLASTIC
DETERGENT

Sulphur

Sulphur is a non-metallic substance which is found in rocks. It is used for making match-heads. Here are the top sulphur producers.

U.S.A.
7,326 thousand tonnes a year
POLAND
4,771 thousand tonnes a year
U.S.S.R.
2,500 thousand tonnes a year

Salt

These countries are the top producers of salt.

U.S.A. 38 million tonnes a year
CHINA 31 million tonnes a year
U.S.S.R. 13 million tonnes a year

7

Natural products

Some plants and animals produce valuable raw materials for industry. Although man-made fibres have now been invented, many fabrics and ropes are still made out of natural fibres, such as cotton, flax, wool and silk. Other natural products, such as wood and rubber, are used to make lots of things too. Many of these natural products grow well in hot climates. They are often the main source of wealth of some poorer countries.

Where does cotton come from?

Cotton comes from the fluffy down which covers the seeds of the cotton plant. These countries produce the most:

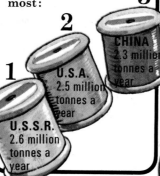

1 U.S.S.R. 2.6 million tonnes a year

2 U.S.A. 2.5 million tonnes a year

3 CHINA 2.3 million tonnes a year

With the wool produced in a year in Australia, you could knit a scarf that would stretch nearly 100 times around the world.

Who produces the most wool?

Wool is the soft, curly coat of sheep. Here are the countries which produce the most:

AUSTRALIA 754 thousand tonnes a year

U.S.S.R. 431 thousand tonnes a year

NEW ZEALAND 312 thousand tonnes a year

The secret of making silk was guarded by the Chinese for 3,000 years. In the sixth century, silkworms were smuggled out of China in a hollow walking stick, and taken to Byzantium (modern Istanbul).

Who produces silk?

Silk is a thread spun by silkworms when they make their cocoons. Here are the top producers:

SOUTH KOREA 4 thousand tonnes a year

CHINA 15 thousand tonnes a year

JAPAN 20 thousand tonnes a year

The greatest lumberjacks

There are two different kinds of wood: softwood, which comes from conifer trees, and hardwood, which comes from broadleaved trees. Here are the top producers of each:

Softwoods

Softwoods, such as pine, fir and spruce, grow in cool climates. Large quantities are made into pulp for making paper.

Top softwood producers are:

1 U.S.S.R. 324 million cubic metres a year

2 U.S.A. 226 million cubic metres a year

3 CANADA 110 million cubic metres a year

The pulp from one tree makes only 3,000 newspapers. One of Britain's daily newspapers sells over 20 million copies every day.

Hardwoods

Hardwoods such as oak and teak, are very strong. They are used for making furniture, boats and houses.

The most valuable hardwoods, such as mahogany and ebony, are found only in tropical forests.

Top hardwood producers are:

3 INDIA 122 million cubic metres a year

2 INDONESIA 130 million cubic metres a year

One mature softwood tree (about 70 years old) contains about ¾ cubic metre of wood.

Who produces the other natural fibres?

Flax
Linen cloth is made from fibres from the stems of the flax plant. It was one of the first fabrics ever made. The top flax growers are:

U.S.S.R.
503 thousand tonnes a year

POLAND
52 thousand tonnes a year

FRANCE
42 thousand tonnes a year

Hemp
The fibres in the stem of the hemp plant are used to make tough fabrics like canvas, sailcloth and rope. Most hemp comes from:

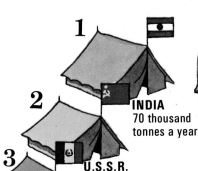

1 INDIA
70 thousand tonnes a year

2 U.S.S.R.
60 thousand tonnes a year

3 ROMANIA
26 thousand tonnes a year

Jute
Fibres from the bark of the jute plant are made into sacking and hessian. It grows only in tropical countries. The top producers are:

CHINA
1.4 million tonnes a year

INDIA
1.1 million tonnes a year

THAILAND
0.2 million tonnes a year

Sisal
Sisal is a strong fibre which comes from the leaves of a special plant. It is used to make ropes. Top producers are:

BRAZIL
167 thousand tonnes a year

TANZANIA
100 thousand tonnes a year

ANGOLA
65 thousand tonnes

Coir
Coir comes from the outer shell of coconuts, and is used for making mats and ropes. Most coir comes from:

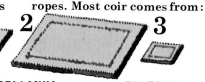

1 INDIA
160 thousand tonnes a year

2 SRI LANKA
100 thousand tonnes a year

3 TANZANIA
6 thousand tonnes a year

Spices, leather and furs

Pepper comes from the fruit of a tropical shrub, grown mainly in Indonesia, Malaysia and India.

Mohair wool, from the Angora goat, comes from South Africa, Lesotho and Texas in the U.S.A.

China produces most camel hair, which is used for the finest paint brushes.

Furs, like mink, sable and ermine, come from Canada and the U.S.S.R.

The U.S.A. produces most leather, but most sheepskins come from the U.S.S.R.

Who grows the most tobacco?

The tobacco plant is related to the tomato and potato plants. It was first brought to Europe 500 years ago by a Spaniard. These countries grow most tobacco.

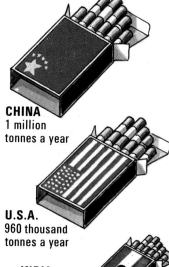

CHINA
1 million tonnes a year

U.S.A.
960 thousand tonnes a year

INDIA
347 thousand tonnes a year

Did you know?

Thousands of fruits and flowers are made into "oil essences" for making perfume. About 600 tonnes of rose petals go into one small bottle of rose-based perfume.

The best rubber growers

Rubber comes from the sap of a special kind of tree, which grows only in hot, wet places. Here are the top rubber producers:

1 BRAZIL
140 million cubic metres a year

One mature hardwood tree (about 120 years old) contains about 1¼ cubic metres of wood.

THAILAND
418 thousand tonnes a year

INDONESIA
850 thousand tonnes a year

MALAYSIA
1½ million tonnes a year
Enough to make tyres for about 58 million cars.

Who grows the most flowers?

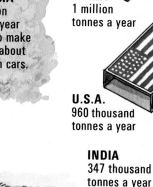

Over 2,700 million flowers are grown, picked and sold each year by the Netherlands.

Where things are made

Who made the most 50 years ago?

Cars

U.S.A. 3.8 million	**GERMANY** 0.1 million
CANADA 0.2 million	**DENMARK** 0.01 million

Ships

U.K. 1.4 million gross reg. tonnes
GERMANY 0.4 gross reg. tonnes
NETHERLANDS 0.2 gross reg. tonnes

Who makes the most aeroplanes?

France is the second highest producer of planes, with about 760 a year.

The U.S.A. builds more commercial aeroplanes than any other country in the world. Over 15,000 planes are built there in a year.

Who makes the most cars?

U.S.A. 6½ million cars a year   **JAPAN** 4½ million cars a year   **FRANCE** 3 million cars a year   **WEST GERMANY** 3 million cars a year

There is one car produced every 5 seconds in the U.S.A.

These countries make the most lorries:

JAPAN 2.4 million a year   **U.S.A.** 2.3 million a year   **U.S.S.R.** 0.8 million a year   **U.K.** 0.4 million a year

These countries make the most motorbikes:

JAPAN 3.8 million a year   **U.S.S.R.** 1 million a year   **FRANCE** 1 million a year   **ITALY** 0.8 million a year

Who makes the most rubber tyres?

U.S.A. 208 million a year (Enough tyres for 52 million cars.)

JAPAN 89 million tyres a year   **FRANCE** 43 million tyres a year   **WEST GERMANY** 38 million a year

Who makes the most ships?

The shipbuilding industry needs huge amounts of steel, so is usually found close to steel factories and to a sheltered coastline. These countries make the most ships.

JAPAN 18 million gross reg. tonnes (which is equivalent to about 51 large tankers)

WEST GERMANY 2.5 million gross reg. tonnes a year   **SWEDEN** 2.4 million gross reg. tonnes a year   **SPAIN** 1.6 million gross reg tonnes a year

Food and drink

By the year 2000, we will have to produce three times as much food as we do at the moment to feed everyone properly. Countries where the soil and climate are good can grow much more food than dry or cold countries. Modern machines, fertilizers and insecticides help farmers to produce more food, but only people in rich countries have enough money to buy them.

Champion meat producers

Here are the top producers of each kind of meat.

BEEF AND VEAL

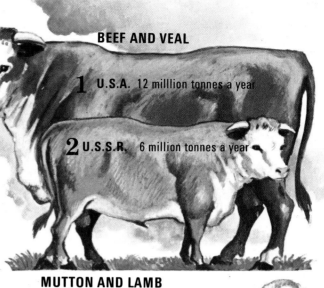

1 U.S.A. 12 million tonnes a year

2 U.S.S.R. 6 million tonnes a year

3 ARGENTINA 3 million tonnes a year

PORK AND BACON

1 CHINA 10 million tonnes a year

2 U.S.A. 6 million tonnes a year

MUTTON AND LAMB

1 U.S.S.R. 900 thousand tonnes a year

2 AUSTRALIA 584 thousand tonnes a year

3 NEW ZEALAND 509 thousand tonnes a year

3 U.S.S.R. 4½ million tonnes a year

POULTRY MEAT

1 U.S.A. 7 million tonnes a year

2 CHINA 3 million tonnes a year

3 U.S.S.R. 1½ million tonnes a year

Who produces the most dairy foods?

Milk (in millions of tonnes a year)

U.S.S.R. 89 U.S.A. 55 FRANCE 30

Butter (in thousands of tonnes a year)

U.S.S.R. 1,263 W. GERMANY 545 FRANCE 544

Cheese (in thousands of tonnes a year)

U.S.A. 1,786 U.S.S.R. 1,435 FRANCE 967

Eggs (in millions of tonnes a year)

U.S.A. 3.8 CHINA 3.7 U.S.S.R. 3.0

Over 2,000 eggs are laid every second in the U.S.A.

Who catches the most fish?

1 JAPAN 10½ million tonnes a year

2 U.S.S.R. 10 million tonnes a year

3 CHINA 7 million tonnes a year

How much can a farmer grow?

Farmers in Canada can feed at least 11 families with the food they produce.

In Africa, many farmers grow only enough food to feed one other family besides their own.

Who produces the most sweet things?

Sugar Cane
INDIA 143 million tonnes a year

Sugar Beet
U.S.S.R. 99 million tonnes a year

Chocolate
U.S.A. 863 thousand tonnes a year

Honey
CHINA 236 thousand tonnes a year

The Swiss are top chocolate eaters—enough chocolate is sold there for them each to eat 2 big bars a day.

How much do people eat?

To keep our bodies fit and healthy, we need foods that contain protein, carbohydrates, fats and vitamins. We can only get enough of these if we eat a good variety of foods. Less than half the people in the world can afford to feed themselves properly.

An Indian farmer eats
about 600g of food a day.
This includes:
480g of rice
2g of meat and dairy foods

An American worker eats
about 2,100g of food a day.
This includes:
325g of bread and potatoes
900g of meat and dairy foods

Why do we need different foods?

Protein

MEAT
FISH
CHEESE
EGGS
SOYA BEANS

Protein is needed for building muscles and keeping bones healthy.

Vitamins

FRUITS
VEGETABLES
OILS

Vitamins help the body resist diseases and keep healthy.

Carbohydrates

BREAD
RICE
POTATOES
SUGAR

Foods containing carbohydrates and fats give us energy and keep us warm.

Top drinks producers

COFFEE

BRAZIL 1.2 million tonnes a year

TEA
INDIA ½ million tonnes a year

WINE
FRANCE 7,500 million litres a year

BEER
U.S.A. 19,000 million litres a year

Top drinkers

COFFEE

SWEDEN 13kg each a year (about 11 cups a day)

TEA
GREAT BRITAIN 4kg each a year (about 5 cups a day)

WINE

PORTUGAL 120 litres each a year

BEER
W. GERMANY 148 litres each a year

Protein from vegetables

Vegetables such as soya-beans and lentils contain some protein and are much cheaper to produce than meat. In the poorer countries they are often the only kind of protein people can get. Here are the top growers of some of these vegetables.

Lentils (in thousands of tonnes a year)

INDIA 460
TURKEY 225
U.S.S.R. 90

Soya Beans (in millions of tonnes a year)

U.S.A. 34
CHINA 12
BRAZIL 11

Cassava (in millions of tonnes a year)

INDONESIA 12½
THAILAND 9
NIGERIA 11

Who grows the most cereals?

Wheat and maize are made into bread, pasta, and breakfast cereals—basic foods in Europe and North America. Boiled or steamed rice is the basic food of most people in Asia. Below are the countries which grow most of these three cereals every year.

Wheat

U.S.S.R. 97 million tonnes a year

U.S.A. 58 million tonnes a year

CHINA 43 million tonnes a year

Rice

CHINA 117 million tonnes a year

INDIA 70½ million tonnes a year

INDONESIA 23 million tonnes a year

Maize

U.S.A. 158 million tonnes a year

CHINA 34 million tonnes a year

BRAZIL 18 million tonnes a year

Where do fruit and vegetables come from?

Fast, refrigerated ships can now carry fresh fruit and vegetables all over the world. Here are some of the top producers.

Apples
U.S.A.
3 million tonnes a year

Bananas
BRAZIL
8 million tonnes a year

Oranges
U.S.A.
10 million tonnes a year

Pineapples
INDIA
850 thousand tonnes a year

Pears
ITALY
1½ million tonnes a year

Lemons
U.S.A. ITALY
780 thousand tonnes each a year

Peaches
U.S.A.
ITALY
1.2 million tonnes each a year

Coconuts
PHILIPPINES
12 million tonnes a year

Tomatoes
TRINIDAD & TOBAGO
7 million tonnes a year

Cabbages
CHINA
5 million tonnes a year

Grapes
FRANCE
10½ million tonnes a year

Cities

About a third of all the people in the world live in towns and cities. Many big modern cities have grown because large numbers of people have moved to live near the factories and offices where they work.

In Africa and Asia most people still live and work on the land. As their industry grows, so will their towns. Experts think that by the year 2000, over half the world's people will live in cities.

The biggest cities in the world

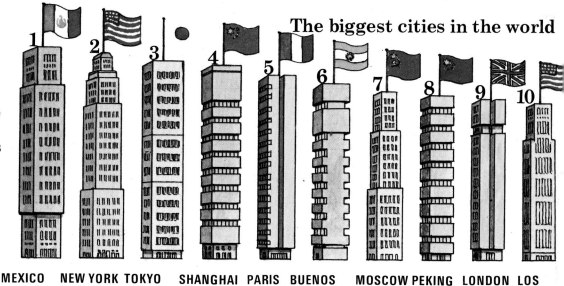

1	2	3	4	5	6	7	8	9	10
MEXICO CITY (MEXICO) 11,943,000 people	NEW YORK (U.S.A.) 11,572,000 people	TOKYO (JAPAN) 11,282,000 people	SHANGHAI (CHINA) 10,820,000 people	PARIS (FRANCE) 9,863,000 people	BUENOS AIRES (ARGENTINA) 8,436,000 people	MOSCOW (U.S.S.R.) 7,734,000 people	PEKING (CHINA) 7,570,000 people	LONDON (UNITED KINGDOM) 7,167,600 people	LOS ANGELES (U.S.A.) 7,032,000 people

Did you know?

There are nearly three times as many people living in Mexico City as there are in the whole of Norway.

The first city

The remains of the oldest city in the world have been found near Jericho in the Israeli occupied territory near the River Jordan. Historians think that about 3,000 people lived there in 7800 BC.

How many big cities are there?

50 YEARS AGO

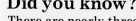

There were 100 cities with more than half a million people.

TODAY

There are over 350 cities with more than half a million people.

Which city has the largest area?

Mount Isa in Queensland, Australia, covers a larger area than any other town in the world. It stretches over 42,000 sq km, and is nearly as big as Switzerland, though Switzerland has 198 times more people.

How many people live in cities?

In America, 11 out of 15 people live in towns, 4 out of 15 people live in the country.

In India, 3 out of 15 people live in towns, 12 out of 15 people live in the country.

What is a city?

A city is usually any large important town, but some small towns which have a cathedral are also called cities. In England, cities are usually towns which have been given a royal "charter" by the king or queen.

What is a capital?

A country's "capital" is its most important, and often its largest, city. It is usually the centre of government and administration.

Which city is growing the fastest?

Mexico City is growing faster than any other city in the world. By the year 2000, experts think that over $31\frac{1}{2}$ million people will be living there—over $2\frac{1}{2}$ times the number living there now.

Did you know?

London has the largest shoe shop in the world. It is Lilley and Skinner's in Oxford Street, where there are 125,000 pairs of shoes in stock.

How old are our cities?

Athens, the capital city of Greece, was the centre of the ancient Greek civilisation 3,000 years ago.

According to legend, Rome was founded in 753 BC by twin boys who had been brought up by a wolf.

Damascus, the capital of Syria, is 4,500 years old, and is the oldest continuously lived in city.

Brasilia was built specially to be Brazil's new capital, and is only about 20 years old.

Some cities and what they are famous for

Zurich in Switzerland is the centre of world banking and finance.

The Hague in the Netherlands is the centre of international law, and the home of the International Court of Justice.

Geneva in Switzerland is the home of the Red Cross. Many international peace conferences are held there.

Oxford and Cambridge in England are world centres of learning. The University of Oxford was founded in the 12th century, and that of Cambridge in the 13th.

Which cities have the biggest?

Hospital

The District Medical Centre in Chicago, U.S.A. is the largest hospital in the world with 5,600 beds.

Football stadium

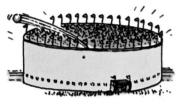

Rio de Janeiro in Brazil has the world's largest football stadium. It is called the Maracana Municipal Stadium and can hold 205,000 people.

Sewage works

The West-Southwest Treatment Plant in Chicago, deals with 4,000 million litres of waste a day—over 57 litres per person.

Museum

The American Museum of Natural History in New York City is the largest museum in the world.

Department store

Macy's in New York is the largest department store in the world.

Which city has most traffic?

In 1977, Hong Kong had 190,746 vehicles and only 1,085km of road. If all these vehicles were on the road at once, there would be about a metre between them.

Which city has the tallest building?

Most cities have had to build very tall buildings as they are short of space. The tallest inhabited building is the Sears Roebuck and Co. office in Chicago which is 443m high. It is shown here next to the Eiffel Tower, the world's tallest building until 1929.

Famous Buildings

The Taj Mahal
In Agra, India. Built between 1631 and 1645 by Emperor Shah Jahan as a tomb for his wife.

The Eiffel Tower
In Paris, France. Built by A. G. Eiffel for a big exhibition in 1889.

The Pyramids
At Giza near Cairo, Egypt. Built about 2500BC as tombs for some of the kings of ancient Egypt.

Big Ben
In London, England. Built in 1834. Named after Benjamin Hall who was in charge of the building.

St Basil's Cathedral
In Moscow, U.S.S.R. Built in the 16th century by the Tsar, Ivan "the Terrible".

Leaning Tower
In Pisa, Italy. Built between 1174 and 1350 as clock tower for nearby cathedral. Upright when built.

Communications

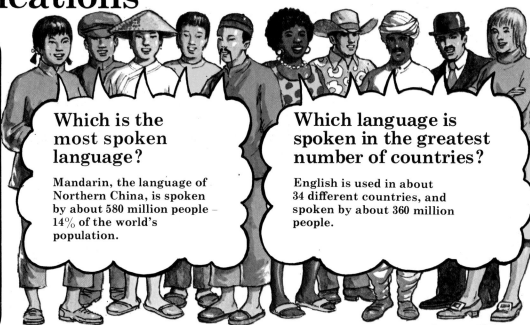

Universal language

About 100 years ago, a Polish doctor invented an international language, called *Esperanto*, which he hoped everyone would learn how to speak. Its words are based on those of European languages, and its grammar is very simple. The name was the doctor's pen-name, and means the "hoping-one". However, there are only about a million people who can speak it.

Which is the most spoken language?

Mandarin, the language of Northern China, is spoken by about 580 million people – 14% of the world's population.

Which language is spoken in the greatest number of countries?

English is used in about 34 different countries, and spoken by about 360 million people.

Who invented writing?

The oldest known writing is Sumerian, dating from around 3500 BC. The land of Sumer was roughly where Iraq is today. Pictures, carved in wet clay, were used as symbols for different words.

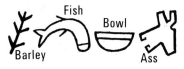

Fish
Bowl
Barley
Ass

Chinese writing still uses picture signs, called "characters". There are over 8,000 different characters.

説 人 賊 狗

How many alphabets are there?

An alphabet is a set of symbols which stand for the sounds we make when we speak. Different sets of symbols are used for different languages. There are about 64 alphabets in use in the world today. Some examples are:

Α ΒΓΔΕ
GREEK

АБВГД
RUSSIAN

Which country has the most languages?

India has the most languages. Of the 4,400 different languages in the world, India has about 845.

The first stamps

The first postage stamps came into use on 6 May 1840 in the United Kingdom. They showed a picture of Queen Victoria, and were called Penny Blacks and Twopenny Blues.

You could make friends with someone in another country by writing to them. On page 32 there are some addresses of organizations which can help you find a pen-friend.

Drum messages

In Zaire, the Congo and other countries in west and central Africa, drums are sometimes used to send messages from one village to another. High and low drum beats and different rhythms are used to send different messages. Each message is repeated about four times to make sure it has been understood. The drums can be heard up to 16 km away.

Who writes the most letters?

U.S.A.
89 thousand million letters a year

JAPAN
13 thousand million letters a year

WEST GERMANY
12 thousand million letters a year.

Who sends the most telegrams?

MEXICO
45 million telegrams a year

U.S.A.
41 million telegrams a year

U.S.S.R. 443 million telegrams a year

Unusual postal systems

One of the earliest kinds of postal system was a "pigeon post", used especially in China.

During the seige of Paris in 1870–71, pigeons were used to carry news into the town from the outside world.

In Peru, there apparently used to be a "swimmer post". Postmen tied the letters on to their heads and swam up and down the rivers in the jungle to deliver the letters.

During the 19th century, postmen in the Landes and Gironde districts of France walked on stilts to deliver the post, to avoid the tall heather which grows there.

Which country has the most daily newspapers?

These countries have the most daily newspapers:

U.S.A. 1,798 different newspapers a day

INDIA 822 different news papers a day

U.S.S.R. 675 different newspapers a day

TURKEY 450 different newspapers a day

In China, news sheets are pasted on to walls where people can read them for free, or have the news read out to them.

Which people have the most telephones?

In rich countries most people have a telephone.

MONACO 84 people out of 100 have a telephone

U.S.A. 70 people out of 100 have a telephone

SWEDEN 66 people out of 100 have a telephone

 In **BANGLADESH**, only 1 person out of 1000 has a telephone

Which people have the most radios?

In the **U.S.A.** most people have 2 radios each

In **CANADA**, 894 people out of 1000 have a radio

In **AFGHANISTAN** and **NEPAL**, only 6 out of 1000 people have a radio

In **NEW ZEALAND**, 892 people out of 1000 have a radio

Who has the most televisions?

In the countries shown here most people have a television. In poor countries, villages sometimes have one communal television for the whole village to watch.

CANADA 366 people out of 1000 have a television

MONACO 607 people out of 1000 have a television

U.S.A. 571 people out of 1000 have a television

 ZAIRE Only 1 person out of 1000 has a television

Which country makes the most films?

Hollywood in California, U.S.A. is often thought to be the centre of the film industry, but these countries make the most films:

1 INDIA 475 films a year

2 JAPAN 405 films a year

3 FRANCE 234 films a year

Which countries have most cinemas?

The first cinema was opened in a Los Angeles circus in the U.S.A. in 1902. Today there are thousands of cinemas throughout the world. These countries have the most:

U.S.S.R. 154,800 cinemas

U.S.A. 14,950 cinemas

ITALY 12,656 cinemas

17

Travel

It took Christopher Columbus ten weeks to travel from Spain to the West Indies in 1492. Today we can travel the same distance in just a few hours. Vast networks of roads, railways, ships and aeroplanes now connect all the countries of the world.

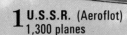

1 U.S.S.R. (Aeroflot) 1,300 planes

2 U.S.A. (T.W.A.) 255 planes

Where is the largest airport in the world?

The largest airport in the world is Dallas, Fort Worth, in Texas, U.S.A. It covers 7,080 hectares, which is bigger than 6,500 football pitches put together.

Which nationality flies the most?

If you look on the luggage tickets you will see which nationalities fly the most in a year.

U.S.A. 223 million passengers

U.S.S.R. 101 million passengers

JAPAN 30 million passengers

U.K. 19 million passengers

Which countries have the most roads?

The U.S.A. has 6 million km of road

CANADA has 3 million km of road

U.S.S.R. has 1.4 million km of road

BRAZIL has 1.3 million km of road

The U.S.A. has enough road to stretch around the world nearly 153 times.

Which countries have the most cars?

In the richer countries, most families own a car. Here are the top four car-owning countries.

U.S.A. 107 million cars
WEST GERMANY 18 million cars
JAPAN 17 million cars
FRANCE 15 million cars

Where is the widest road?

The widest road in the world is the Monumental Axis, in Brazil. It is 250 metres wide, and you could fit 160 cars across it side by side.

Where is the narrowest street?

St John's Lane in Rome, Italy, is probably the narrowest street in the world. It is 48cm wide—only just wider than this book when it is open.

Which nationality has most holidays abroad?

Many people now go to foreign countries for their holidays. These nationalities are the top travellers to the popular tourist countries.

35 million West Germans a year

12 million French people a year

10 million Canadians a year

4 million Belgians a year

Which side of the road do people drive on?

99 countries drive on the right.

42 countries drive on the left.

Who makes the biggest plane?

The heaviest, largest and most powerful plane is the U.S.A. "Jumbo" jet, or Boeing 747, which can carry up to 500 passengers. It weighs 381 tonnes—as much as 67 African elephants. There are 313 Jumbo jets in operation, of which Pan Am has 39.

4 FRANCE (Air France) 131 planes

6 U.S.A. (Pan Am) 102 planes

9 ITALY (Al Italia) 65 planes

5 CANADA (Air Canada) 120 planes

7 GERMANY (Lufthansa) 91 planes

3 U.K. (British Airways) 201 planes

10 NETHERLANDS (K.L.M.) 48 planes

8 JAPAN (Japan Air Lines) 75 planes

Which is the fastest way to travel?

Where is the busiest airport?

The busiest airport in the world is Chicago International Airport, Illinois, U.S.A. which has a plane taking off or landing every 45 seconds, 24 hours a day.

The fastest passenger vehicle in the world is *Concorde*, which travels faster than the speed of sound, cruising at 2,170 k.p.h. It can fly across the Atlantic in just over three hours. British Airways operates five of them, and Air France four.

How far is it between the world's big cities?

Here is a chart showing the distance and flying times between six large cities, chosen from all round the world.

How to use this chart: Find the column going down the chart for one city, and the row going across the chart for the other city. The box where the two rows cross will give you the distances and flying time between the two cities.

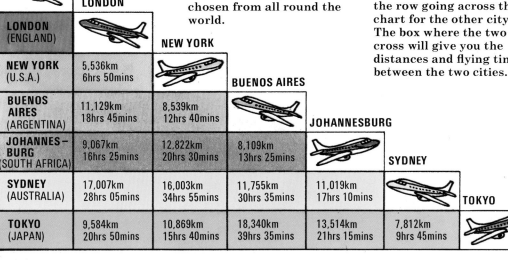

	LONDON	NEW YORK	BUENOS AIRES	JOHANNESBURG	SYDNEY	TOKYO
LONDON (ENGLAND)						
NEW YORK (U.S.A.)	5,536km 6hrs 50mins					
BUENOS AIRES (ARGENTINA)	11,129km 18hrs 45mins	8,539km 12hrs 40mins				
JOHANNES-BURG (SOUTH AFRICA)	9,067km 16hrs 25mins	12,822km 20hrs 30mins	8,109km 13hrs 25mins			
SYDNEY (AUSTRALIA)	17,007km 28hrs 05mins	16,003km 34hrs 55mins	11,755km 30hrs 35mins	11,019km 17hrs 10mins		
TOKYO (JAPAN)	9,584km 20hrs 50mins	10,869km 15hrs 40mins	18,340km 39hrs 35mins	13,514km 21hrs 15mins	7,812km 9hrs 45mins	

Travelling by sea

Few people travel by sea, except for pleasure, as it is expensive and slow. However, most cargo is still sent by sea, in ships built specially to hold different kinds of goods.

The largest cargo ships

The largest ships in the world are two French-built oil tankers. They can each carry 553,662 tonnes of cargo, and are 400 m long—nearly as long as the Sydney Harbour Bridge.

Which is the largest passenger ship?

The largest passenger ship in the world is the *Queen Elizabeth II*, which sails under the British flag. It has 920 bedrooms, and can carry 1,800 passengers. Buckingham Palace, home of Queen Elizabeth II, has only 600 rooms.

Which countries have most railway track?

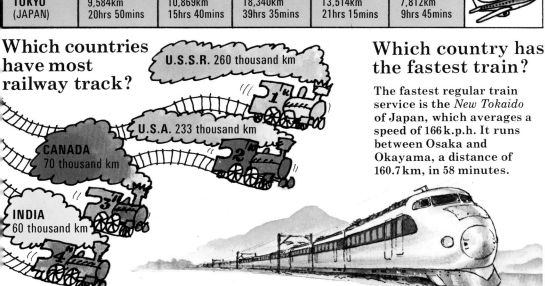

U.S.S.R. 260 thousand km

U.S.A. 233 thousand km

CANADA 70 thousand km

INDIA 60 thousand km

Which country has the fastest train?

The fastest regular train service is the *New Tokaido* of Japan, which averages a speed of 166 k.p.h. It runs between Osaka and Okayama, a distance of 160.7 km, in 58 minutes.

Weather

Though the weather changes each day, the general pattern of temperature and rainfall is fairly similar year after year. This weather pattern is called climate. A country's climate depends on its position on the globe, its height above sea level, distance from the sea and local winds.

Where is the sunniest place in the world?

The sun shines almost all day, every day in the Sahara Desert in the Sudan. There are only about 80 hours a year when it is cloudy during the day.

Where is the most thundery place in the world?

The island of Java, in Indonesia, has about 322 thundery days a year. Altogether there are about 45,000 thunderstorms in the world every day.

Where was the worst hail storm?

Hailstones the size of cannon balls fell on Coffeyville, a town in Kansas, U.S.A. in 1970. They were 19 cm across (about the width of this page) and weighed ¾ kg.

Which are the hottest countries?

The countries which have the highest average temperatures throughout the year are mostly the hot desert lands. Here are the three hottest countries.

NIGER 27.8°C

MALI 28.3°C

UPPER VOLTA 28.1°C

Where are the coldest places?

Lands near the North and South Poles are the coldest places on Earth. Some are covered in thick ice throughout the year, as the sun never rises very high in the sky. The coldest lands in the world are:

The coldest temperature ever recorded is −88°C in Vostok, Antarctica in 1960. That is 67° colder than the temperature inside a deep freeze.

ANTARCTICA (International Territory) −60°C

GREENLAND (Territory of Denmark) −7.3°C

ALASKA (U.S.A.) −1.2°C

It was so cold in Canada in 1925 that the Niagara Falls were completely frozen.

Which are the driest countries?

Large areas of some countries are covered by deserts, where there is sometimes no rain for several years. Very few things can live or grow there because there is so little water. These are the driest countries in the world.

EGYPT 55.8mm of rain a year.

SAUDI ARABIA 73.6mm of rain a year

MAURITANIA 82.8mm of rain a year

This is the actual depth of rain Egypt gets in a year.

Which are the wettest countries?

Countries near the equator, especially those near the sea, have heavy rainstorms nearly every day. Great forests grow in these hot wet countries. More rain falls in these countries in a year than in any others.

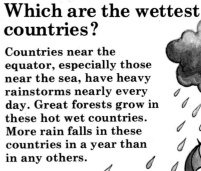

SIERRA LEONE 2,829mm of rain a year

MALAYSIA 3,273mm of rain a year

COLOMBIA 4,099mm of rain a year

Where was the worst snow storm?

During five days of 1958, over 4 m of snow fell on the Thompson Pass in Alaska, U.S.A. This much snow would almost bury a giraffe.

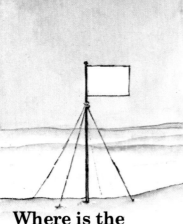

Where is the least sunny place in the world?

During the winter, the South Pole, in Antarctica, has no sun at all for nearly 27 weeks.

Where is the driest place in the world?

The longest drought was in the Atacama Desert in Chile. Until 1971, it had not rained there for 400 years, making it the driest place in the world.

Where is the wettest place in the world?

There are only about six days a year when it does not rain on Mount Wai-'ale'ale in Hawaii.

Great winds

Tornado

The worst tornado ever recorded swept across Texas, U.S.A. in 1958. It travelled at 450 k.p.h. — three times faster than the fastest train in the world.

Hurricane

Hurricanes are violent winds which blow in huge spirals over warm seas. The Gulf of Mexico and the West Indies are hit by hurricanes about 11 times a year.

Monsoon

Monsoon winds blow over the tropical countries of Asia. In winter, they blow out to sea but in summer they blow inland, bringing heavy rains. This is the "monsoon" season.

1

There are usually lines drawn round globes, called lines of latitude. The one round the middle is called 0° Latitude, or the equator.

2

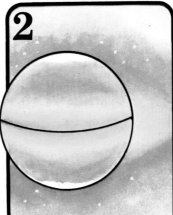

Countries near the equator are usually the hottest. Countries with higher latitude numbers are usually colder.

3

There are about 3½ times as many countries above the equator as there are below.

4

The countries above the equator have winter while the ones below have summer. Countries on the equator are hot all year round. About 104 countries have a hot Christmas Day.

5

Lines of longitude run round the globe longways. You can find the exact position of any place in the world from the numbers of the latitude and longitude lines that run near it.

Time differences

There is one hour's time difference for every 15° change in longitude. Places on the line of 0° Longitude have "Greenwich Mean Time". Travelling west from this line you put your watch back, and travelling east you put it forward.*

Local time in different countries is shown on the chart on pages 28–31.

Natural wonders

Scientists think that the Earth's crust (the layer of rock which covers the surface of the Earth) is made up of several separate pieces called "plates" Earthquakes and volcanoes, caused by movements of these plates, change the shape of the land and have produced many of the world's natural wonders. Wind and water constantly wear away the land, making strange rock shapes, river valleys and waterfalls.

How much of the world is land?

More than two-thirds of the Earth's surface is covered by water, leaving only about a third as land. Most of the land is above the equator.

TOTAL SURFACE AREA: 510,066,100sq km

SEA: 364,340,215sq km

LAND: 145,725,885sq km

Oceans and seas

All the oceans are joined together and you can travel from one to the other without ever crossing any land. The seas are part of the great oceans. These are the world's biggest seas:

MALAY SEA	8,142,000sq km	(Pacific Ocean)
CARIBBEAN SEA	2,753,000sq km	(Atlantic Ocean)
MEDITERRANEAN SEA	2,503,000sq km	(Atlantic Ocean)

ARCTIC OCEAN 13,980,000sq km

INDIAN OCEAN 73,550,000sq km

ATLANTIC OCEAN 82,360,000 sq km

THE SEAS

FERTILE LAND

DESERT

FORESTS

ICE

MOUNTAINS

PACIFIC OCEAN 165,240,000sq km

Where is the biggest cactus?

The *sequeru* cacti of Arizona, U.S.A. and Mexico have branches which grow to a height of 16m—about nine times taller than a man

Where are the largest deserts?

Deserts are places which have less than 250mm of rain a year. These are the largest deserts and the countries they are in.

THE SAHARA 8,400,000sq km

(Algeria, Chad, Egypt, Libya, Mali, Mauritania, Morocco, Niger, Sudan Tunisia.)

The Sahara gets its name from the Arabic word *sahra*, which means wilderness. It is nearly as big as the U.S.A.

AUSTRALIAN DESERT 1,550,000sq km (Australia)

ARABIAN DESERT 1,300,000sq km (Saudi Arabia, North Yemen, South Yemen, Qatar, Oman, United Arab Emirates.)

GOBI DESERT 1,040,000sq km (Mongolia, China)

Where are the longest rivers?

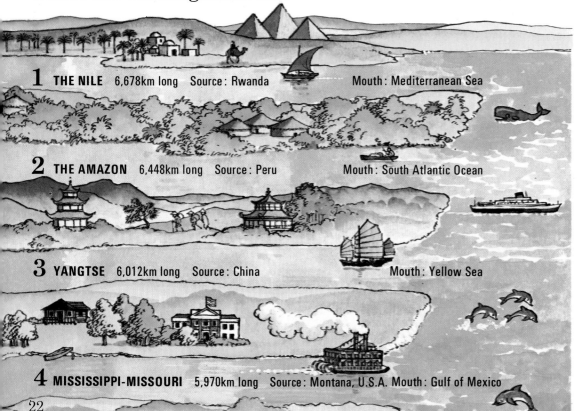

1 THE NILE 6,678km long   Source: Rwanda   Mouth: Mediterranean Sea

2 THE AMAZON 6,448km long   Source: Peru   Mouth: South Atlantic Ocean

3 YANGTSE 6,012km long   Source: China   Mouth: Yellow Sea

4 MISSISSIPPI-MISSOURI 5,970km long   Source: Montana, U.S.A. Mouth: Gulf of Mexico

Where are the highest mountains?

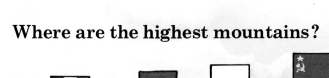

MONT BLANC 4,807m Alps in France (W. Europe)

NGGA PULU 5,029m Pegunungan Maoke in Indonesia (Oceania)

VINSON MASSIF 5,140m Sentinel Range in Antarctica

MOUNT EL'BRUS 5,663m Caucasus in U.S.S.R. (E. Europe)

MOUNT KILIMANJARO 5,894m in Tanzania (Africa)

MOUNT McKINLEY 6,194m Alaska Range in U.S.A. (North America)

MOUNT ACONCAGUA 6,960m Andes in Argentina (South America)

MOUNT EVEREST 8,848m Himalayas in Nepal (Asia) Highest mountain in the world.

The 200 highest mountains in the world are all in the Himalayas. These are the highest mountains in each continent, with their heights, ranges and the countries they are in.

Where are the greatest mountain ranges?

Here are the four longest mountain ranges. They were formed millions of years ago, when rocks were squeezed together by tremendous movements in the Earth's crust.

THE ANDES 7,200km long (Venezuela, Colombia, Ecuador, Peru, Bolivia, Argentina, Chile.)

THE ROCKY MOUNTAINS 6,000km long (U.S.A. and Canada.)

THE HIMALAYA-KARAKORAM-HINDU KUSH-PAMIR RANGE 3,800km long (Bhutan, China, Nepal, India, Pakistan, Afghanistan.)

The most regular geyser is *Old Faithful* in the Yellowstone National Park, U.S.A., which shoots hot water into the air every hour.

THE GREAT DIVIDING RANGE 3,600km long (Australia)

Where was the worst earthquake?

The worst earthquake ever is thought to have been in Shensi Province, China in 1556, when 830,000 people were killed.

Where was the worst volcano?

Probably the greatest volcanic eruption ever was on the island of Santorini, in the Aegean Sea, around 1470BC. Scientists have worked out that it was about 130 times more powerful than the biggest H-Bomb explosion.

Strange places

Mount Kilimanjaro (5,894m) in Tanzania is not part of a mountain range. It is an extinct volcano. Although it is very near the equator, it always has snow on top.

The Grand Canyon in the U.S.A. is over 1,700m deep in places. Shadows made by the sun make the rock appear to change colour.

Where is the tallest waterfall?

The highest waterfall in the world is the Angel Falls in Venezuela, which is 979m high. It is twice as high as the Sears-Roebuck tower—the tallest building in the world.

Where are the largest lakes?

LAKE SUPERIOR 82,400sq km (Canada and U.S.A.)

LAKE VICTORIA 69,500sq km (Uganda, Tanzania and Kenya)

ARAL'SKOYE 65,500sq km (U.S.S.R.)

Where is the tallest tree?

The tallest tree in the world is a Coast Redwood in California, U.S.A. It is 111.6m high—over 63 times taller than a man.

Where the countries are

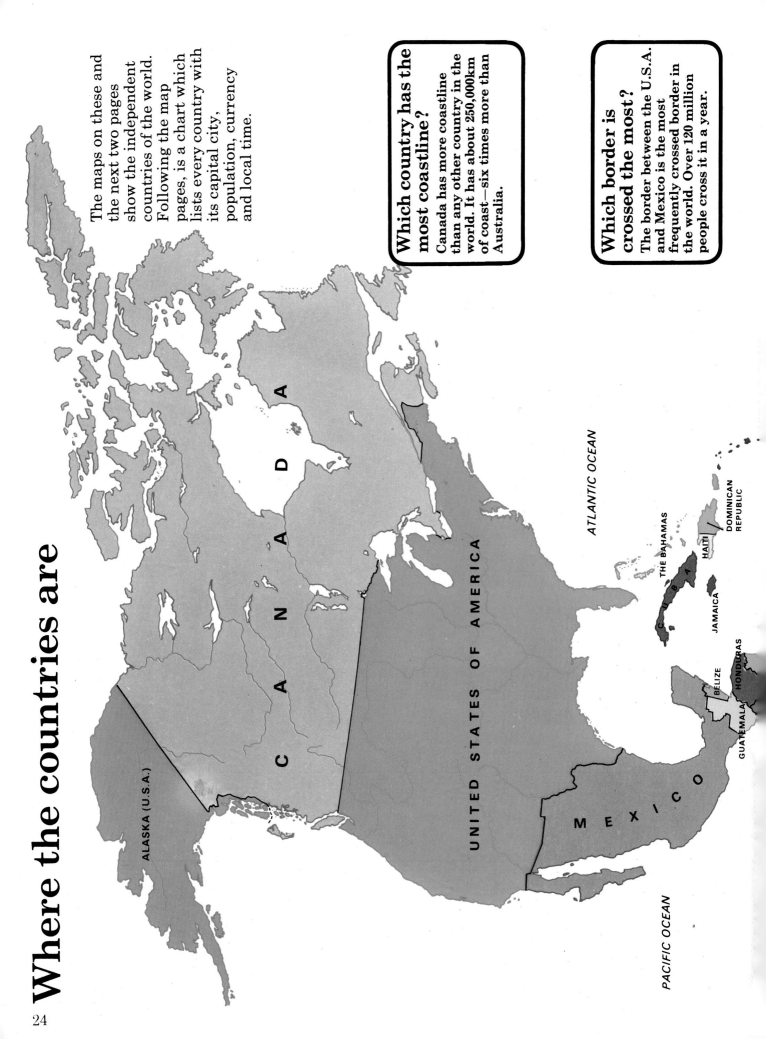

The maps on these and the next two pages show the independent countries of the world. Following the map pages, is a chart which lists every country with its capital city, population, currency and local time.

Which country has the most coastline?
Canada has more coastline than any other country in the world. It has about 250,000km of coast—six times more than Australia.

Which border is crossed the most?
The border between the U.S.A. and Mexico is the most frequently crossed border in the world. Over 120 million people cross it in a year.

CANADA

ALASKA (U.S.A.)

UNITED STATES OF AMERICA

MEXICO

PACIFIC OCEAN

ATLANTIC OCEAN

THE BAHAMAS

CUBA

JAMAICA

HAITI

DOMINICAN REPUBLIC

BELIZE

GUATEMALA

HONDURAS

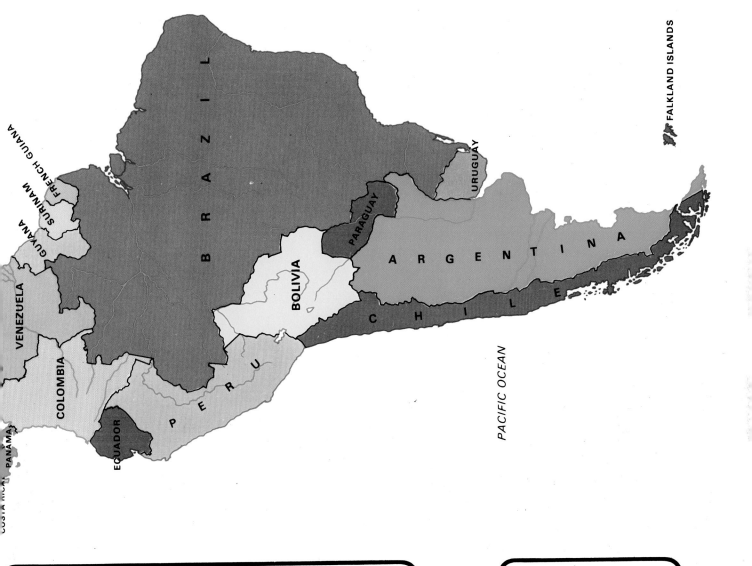

FRENCH GUIANA

SURINAM

GUYANA

VENEZUELA

COLOMBIA

PANAMA

COSTA RICA

ECUADOR

P E R U

B R A Z I L

BOLIVIA

PARAGUAY

URUGUAY

A R G E N T I N A

C H I L E

PACIFIC OCEAN

FALKLAND ISLANDS

What are the states of the U.S.A.?

These are the 50 states of the U.S.A. Each state is represented by a star on the U.S.A. flag.

Alabama
Alaska
Arizona
Arkansas
California
Colorado
Connecticut
Delaware
Florida
Georgia
Hawaii
Idaho
Illinois
Indiana
Iowa
Kansas
Kentucky
Louisiana
Maine
Maryland
Massachusetts
Michigan
Minnesota
Mississippi
Missouri
Montana
Nebraska
Nevada
New Hampshire
New Jersey
New Mexico
New York
North Carolina
North Dakota
Ohio
Oklahoma
Oregon
Pennsylvania
Rhode Island
South Carolina
South Dakota
Tennessee
Texas
Utah
Vermont
Virginia
Washington
West Virginia
Wisconsin
Wyoming

Who owns Antarctica?

Seven countries have made claims to parts of Antarctica, but they have agreed to wait until 1989 before finally deciding on them. The countries involved are: Australia, Argentina, Chile, New Zealand, France, Norway and the United Kingdom.

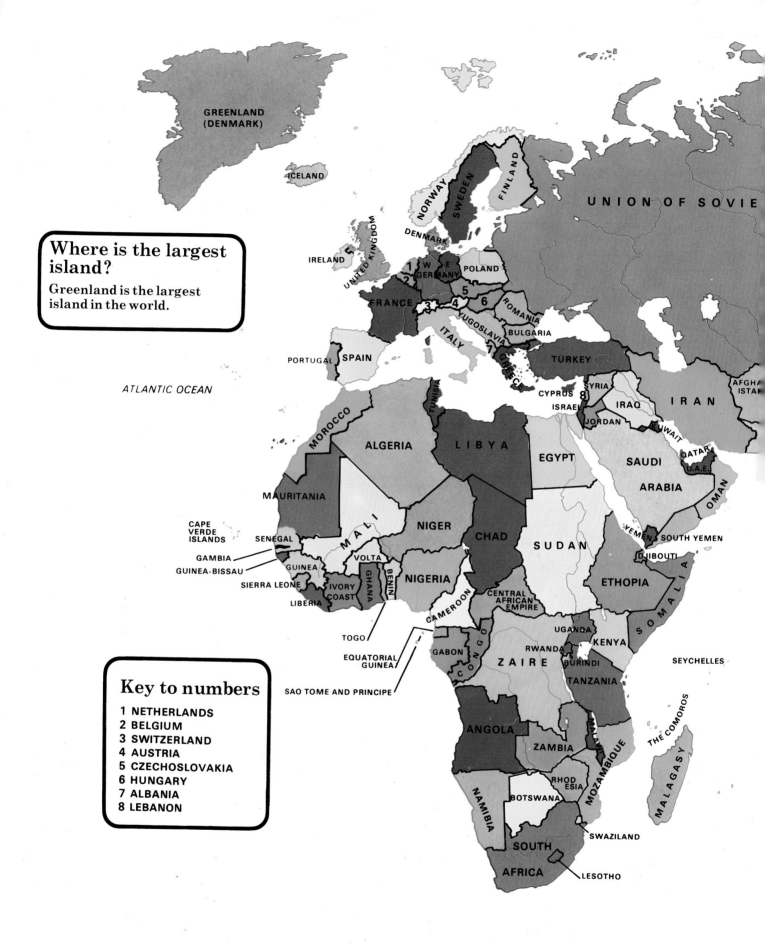

GREENLAND
(DENMARK)

ICELAND

Where is the largest island?

Greenland is the largest island in the world.

ATLANTIC OCEAN

NORWAY
SWEDEN
FINLAND
DENMARK
IRELAND
UNITED KINGDOM
1 W E
GERMANY
POLAND
5
FRANCE
3 4 6
ROMANIA
YUGOSLAVIA
BULGARIA
ITALY
7
PORTUGAL
SPAIN
GREECE
TURKEY
CYPRUS
SYRIA
8
ISRAEL
IRAQ
JORDAN
IRAN
AFGHA
ISTA
KUWAIT
QATAR
U.A.E.
SAUDI
ARABIA
OMAN
MOROCCO
ALGERIA
LIBYA
EGYPT
MAURITANIA
NIGER
CHAD
SUDAN
YEMEN
SOUTH YEMEN
DJIBOUTI
ETHIOPIA
SOMALIA

UNION OF SOVIE

CAPE
VERDE
ISLANDS
SENEGAL
GAMBIA
GUINEA-BISSAU
GUINEA
SIERRA LEONE
LIBERIA
IVORY
COAST
GHANA
BENIN
VOLTA
NIGERIA
MALI
TOGO
EQUATORIAL
GUINEA
SAO TOME AND PRINCIPE
CAMEROON
CENTRAL
AFRICAN
EMPIRE
GABON
CONGO
ZAIRE
UGANDA
RWANDA
BURINDI
KENYA
TANZANIA
SEYCHELLES

Key to numbers

1 NETHERLANDS
2 BELGIUM
3 SWITZERLAND
4 AUSTRIA
5 CZECHOSLOVAKIA
6 HUNGARY
7 ALBANIA
8 LEBANON

ANGOLA
ZAMBIA
MALAWI
MOZAMBIQUE
THE COMOROS
MALAGASY
RHOD
ESIA
NAMIBIA
BOTSWANA
SWAZILAND
SOUTH
AFRICA
LESOTHO

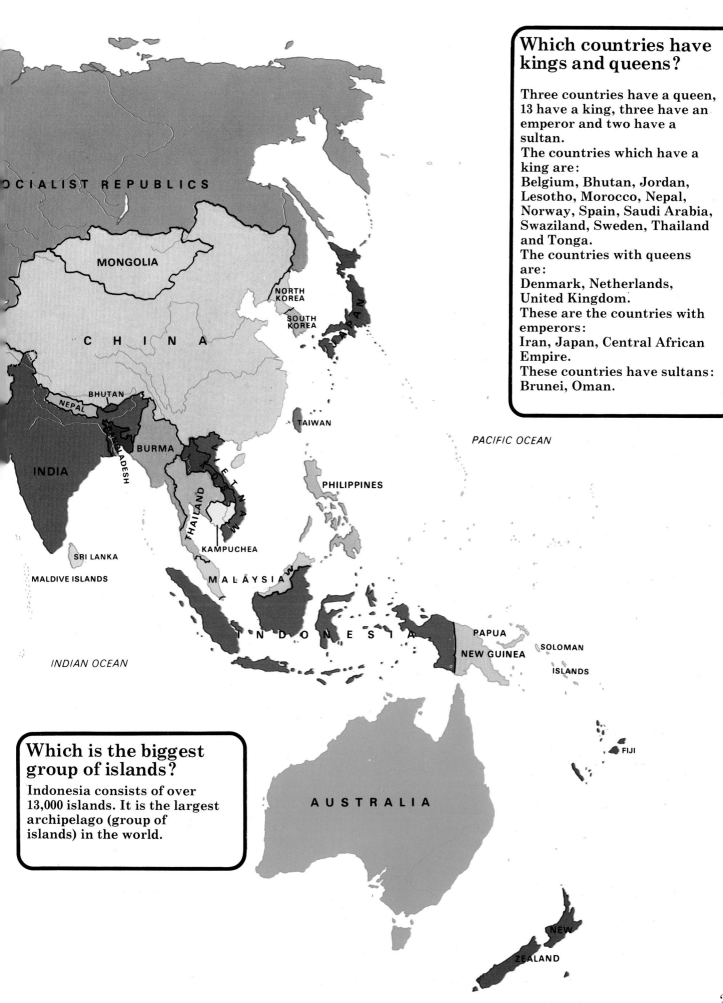

Which countries have kings and queens?

Three countries have a queen, 13 have a king, three have an emperor and two have a sultan.
The countries which have a king are:
Belgium, Bhutan, Jordan, Lesotho, Morocco, Nepal, Norway, Spain, Saudi Arabia, Swaziland, Sweden, Thailand and Tonga.
The countries with queens are:
Denmark, Netherlands, United Kingdom.
These are the countries with emperors:
Iran, Japan, Central African Empire.
These countries have sultans:
Brunei, Oman.

Which is the biggest group of islands?

Indonesia consists of over 13,000 islands. It is the largest archipelago (group of islands) in the world.

PACIFIC OCEAN

INDIAN OCEAN

OCIALIST REPUBLICS

MONGOLIA

NORTH KOREA

SOUTH KOREA

JAPAN

CHINA

BHUTAN

NEPAL

INDIA

BANGLADESH

BURMA

TAIWAN

VIETNAM

THAILAND

KAMPUCHEA

PHILIPPINES

SRI LANKA

MALDIVE ISLANDS

MALAYSIA

INDONESIA

PAPUA NEW GUINEA

SOLOMAN ISLANDS

AUSTRALIA

FIJI

NEW ZEALAND

27

Countries of the world chart

Country name	Population	Capital city	Time in capital (ahead or behind G.M.T.)	Currency
AFGHANISTAN	19,803,000	Kabul	4½ hours ahead	Afghani (100 puls)
ALBANIA	2,548,000	Tirana	1 hour ahead	Lek (100 qintars)
ALGERIA	17,304,000	Algiers	G.M.T.	Algerian dinar (100 centimes)
ANDORRA	26,558	Andorra	G.M.T.	French franc, Spanish peseta
ANGOLA	6,511,000	Luanda	1 hour ahead	Angolan escudo (100 centavos)
ARGENTINA	26,719,000	Buenos Aires	3 hours behind	Peso (100 centavos)
AUSTRALIA	13,642,000	Canberra	10 hours ahead	Australian dollar (100 cents)
AUSTRIA	7,514,000	Vienna	1 hour ahead	Schilling (100 groschen)
BAHAMAS	170,849	Nassau	5 hours behind	Bahamian dollar (100 cents)
BAHRAIN	259,000	Manama	4 hours ahead	Bahraini dinar (1,000 fils)
BANGLADESH	76,815,000	Dacca	6 hours ahead	Taka (100 paisa)
BARBADOS	247,400	Bridgetown	4 hours behind	Barbadian dollar (100 cents)
BELGIUM	9,889,000	Brussels	1 hour ahead	Belgian franc (100 centimes)
BENIN	3,197,000	Porto-Novo	1 hour ahead	African financial community franc
BHUTAN	1,202,000	Thimbu	6 hours ahead	Ngultrum (100 chetrum)
BOLIVIA	5,789,300	La Paz	4 hours behind	Bolivian peso (100 centavos)
BOTSWANA	693,000	Gaberone	2 hours ahead	South African rand
BRAZIL	109,180,600	Brasilia	3 hours behind	Cruzeiro (100 centavos)
BULGARIA	8,760,971	Sofia	2 hours ahead	Lev (100 stotinki)
BURMA	31,002,000	Rangoon	6½ hours ahead	Kyat (100 pyas)
BURUNDI	3,864,000	Bujumbura	2 hours ahead	Burundi franc (100 centimes)
CAMEROON	6,531,000	Yaounde	1 hour ahead	African financial community franc
CANADA	23,140,000	Ottawa	5 hours behind	Canadian dollar (100 cents)
CAPE VERDE ISLANDS	303,066	Praia	1 hour behind	Cape Verde escudo (100 centavos)
CENTRAL AFRICAN EMPIRE	2,370,000	Bangui	1 hour ahead	African financial community franc
CHAD	4,116,000	N'Djamena	1 hour ahead	African financial community franc
CHILE	16,454,387	Santiago	4 hours behind	Chilean peso (100 centavos)
CHINA	852,133,000	Peking	8 hours ahead	Yüan (100 fen)
COLOMBIA	24,372,100	Bogotá	5 hours behind	Colombian peso (100 centavos)
COMOROS	314,000	Moroni	3 hours ahead	African financial community franc
CONGO	1,390,000	Brazzaville	1 hour ahead	African financial community franc
COSTA RICA	2,012,480	San José	6 hours behind	Costa Rican colon (100 céntimos)
CUBA	9,331,977	Havana	5 hours behind	Cuban peso (100 centavos)
CYPRUS	639,000	Nicosia	2 hours ahead	Cypriot pound (1000 mils)
CZECHOSLOVAKIA	14,918,186	Prague	1 hour ahead	Koruna (100 haléru)
DENMARK	5,072,516	Copenhagen	1 hour ahead	Danish krone (100 øre)
DJIBOUTI	104,000	Djibouti	3 hours ahead	Djiboutian franc

Country name	Population	Capital city	Time in capital (ahead or behind G.M.T.)	Currency
DOMINICAN REPUBLIC	4,835,207	Santo Domingo	4 hours behind	Dominican peso (100 centavos)
ECUADOR	7,305,000	Quito	5 hours behind	Sucre (100 centavos)
EGYPT	38,067,000	Cairo	2 hours ahead	Egyptian pound (100 piastres)
EL SALVADOR	4,123,323	San Salvador	6 hours behind	Salvadorean colón (100 centavos)
EQUATORIAL GUINEA	316,000	Malabo	1 hour ahead	Ekuele (100 centimos)
ETHIOPIA	28,667,800	Addis Ababa	3 hours ahead	Ethiopian dollar (100 cents)
FIJI	580,000	Suva	12 hours ahead	Fijian dollar (100 cents)
FINLAND	4,726,616	Helsinki	2 hours ahead	Markka (100 penniä)
FRANCE	52,915,000	Paris	1 hour ahead	French franc (100 centimes)
GABON	530,000	Libreville	1 hour ahead	African financial community franc
GAMBIA	538,200	Banjul	G.M.T.	Dalasi (100 butut)
GERMANY, EAST	16,786,057	East Berlin	1 hour ahead	D.D.R. mark (100 pfennige)
GERMANY, WEST	61,498,000	Bonn	1 hour ahead	Deutschmark (100 pfennige)
GHANA	10,309,007	Accra	G.M.T.	New cedi (100 pesewas)
GREECE	9,165,000	Athens	2 hours ahead	Drachma (100 leptae)
GRENADA	96,000	Saint George's	4 hours behind	East Caribbean dollar (100 cents)
GUATEMALA	6,256,199	Guatemala City	6 hours behind	Quetzal (100 centavos)
GUINEA	4,529,000	Conakry	G.M.T.	Syli (100 cauris)
GUINEA-BISSAU	534,000	Madina do Boé	G.M.T.	Guinea peso (100 centavos)
GUYANA	782,805	Georgetown	3 hours behind	Guanese dollar (100 cents)
HAITI	4,688,162	Port-au-Prince	5 hours behind	Gourde (100 centimes)
HONDURAS	3,141,000	Tegucigalpa	6 hours behind	Lempira (100 centavos)
HUNGARY	10,596,000	Budapest	1 hour ahead	Forint (100 fillér)
ICELAND	220,100	Reykjavik	1 hour behind	Icelandic króna (100 aurar)
INDIA	610,077,000	New Delhi	5½ hours ahead	Rupee (100 paisa)
INDONESIA	139,616,000	Djakarta	7 hours ahead	Rupiah (100 sen)
IRAN	33,900,000	Teheran	3½ hours ahead	Iranian rial (100 dinars)
IRAQ	11,505,234	Baghdad	3 hours ahead	Iraqi dinar (1000 fils)
IRELAND	3,162,000	Dublin	G.M.T.	Irish pound (100 pence)
ISRAEL	3,464,900	Jerusalem	2 hours ahead	Israeli pound (100 agorot)
ITALY	56,189,000	Rome	1 hour ahead	Italian lira
IVORY COAST	5,017,000	Abidjan	G.M.T.	African financial community franc
JAMAICA	2,057,000	Kingston	5 hours behind	Jamaican dollar (100 cents)
JAPAN	112,767,795	Tokyo	9 hours ahead	Yen (100 sen)
JORDAN	2,779,000	Amman	2 hours ahead	Jordanian dinar (1000 fils)
KAMPUCHEA	8,110,000	Phnom-Penh	7 hours ahead	Riel (100 sen)
KENYA	13,847,000	Nairobi	3 hours ahead	Kenyan shilling (100 cents)
KOREA, NORTH	15,852,000	Pyong Yang	9 hours ahead	Won (100 jeon)
KOREA, SOUTH	33,439,000	Seoul	9 hours ahead	Won (100 jeon)
KUWAIT	1,030,500	Kuwait City	3 hours ahead	Kuwaiti dinar (1000 fils)
LAOS	3,383,000	Vientiane	7 hours ahead	Liberaton kip (100 at)
LEBANON	2,961,000	Beirut	2 hours ahead	Lebanese pound (100 piastres)
LESOTHO	1,038,500	Maseru	2 hours ahead	South African rand
LIBERIA	1,751,000	Monrovia	G.M.T.	Liberian dollar (100 cents)

Country name	Population	Capital city	Time in capital (ahead or behind G.M.T.)	Currency
LIBYA	2,444,000	Tripoli	2 hours ahead	Libyan dinar (1000 dirhams)
LIECHTENSTEIN	22,000	Vaduz	1 hour ahead	Swiss franc
LUXEMBOURG	358,000	Luxembourg	1 hour ahead	Luxembourg franc (100 centimes)
MALAGASY	8,266,000	Tananarive	3 hours ahead	Malgache franc (100 centimes)
MALAWI	5,175,000	Lilongwe	2 hours ahead	Malawian kwacha (100 tambala)
MALAYSIA	12,300,000	Kuala Lumpur	8 hours ahead	Ringgit (Malaysian dollar) (100 sen)
MALDIVES	122,000	Malé	5 hours ahead	Maldivian rupee (100 larees)
MALI	5,844,000	Bamako	G.M.T.	Malian franc
MALTA	303,685	Valletta	1 hour ahead	Maltese pound (100 cents)
MAURITANIA	1,318,000	Nouakchott	G.M.T.	Ouguiya (5 khoums)
MAURITIUS	894,774	Port Louis	4 hours ahead	Mauritian rupee (100 cents)
MEXICO	62,329,189	Mexico City	6 hours behind	Mexican peso (100 centavos)
MONACO	23,400	Monaco	1 hour ahead	French franc
MONGOLIA	1,488,000	Ulan Bator	7 hours ahead	Tugrik (100 möngö)
MOROCCO	17,828,000	Rabat	G.M.T.	Dirham (100 centimes)
MOZAMBIQUE	9,444,000	Maputo	2 hours ahead	Mozambican escudo (100 centavos)
NAMIBIA	862,000	Windhoek	1 hour ahead	South African rand
NAURU	7,128	Nauru	11½ hours ahead	Australian dollar
NEPAL	12,857,243	Katmandu	5½ hours ahead	Nepalese rupee (100 paisa)
NETHERLANDS	13,769,913	The Hague	1 hour ahead	Gulden (100 cents)
NEW ZEALAND	3,138,400	Wellington	12 hours ahead	New Zealand dollar (100 cents)
NICARAGUA	2,233,000	Managua	6 hours behind	Cordoba (100 centavos)
NIGER	4,727,292	Niamey	1 hour ahead	African financial community franc
NIGERIA	64,750,000	Lagos	1 hour ahead	Naira (100 kobo)
NORWAY	4,026,000	Oslo	1 hour ahead	Norwegian krone (100 øre)
OMAN	791,000	Muscat	4 hours ahead	Omani rial (100 baiza)
PAKISTAN	72,368,000	Islamabad	5 hours ahead	Pakistani rupee (100 paisa)
PANAMA	1,718,700	Panama	5 hours behind	Balboa (100 centésimos)
PAPUA NEW GUINEA	2,829,000	Port Moresby	10 hours ahead	Kina (100 toea)
PARAGUAY	2,724,392	Asunción	4 hours behind	Guarani (100 céntimos)
PERU	16,090,496	Lima	5 hours behind	Sol (100 centavos)
PHILIPPINES	43,751,320	Quezon City	8 hours ahead	Filipino peso (100 centavos)
POLAND	34,362,133	Warsaw	1 hour ahead	Zloty (100 groszy)
PORTUGAL	9,448,800	Lisbon	1 hour ahead	Portuguese escudo (100 centavos)
QATAR	95,000	Doha	4 hours ahead	Qatar riyal (100 dirhams)
RHODESIA	6,200,000	Salisbury	2 hours ahead	Rhodesian dollar (100 cents)
ROMANIA	21,445,698	Bucharest	2 hours ahead	Leu (100 bani)
RWANDA	4,289,000	Kigali	2 hours ahead	Rwandese franc (100 centimes)
SAN MARINO	19,261	San Marino	1 hour ahead	Italian lira
SAO TOMÉ AND PRINCIPE	81,000	Sao Tomé	G.M.T.	Guinea escudo (100 centavos)
SAUDI ARABIA	9,240,000	Riyadh	3 hours ahead	Saudi riyal (100 halalah)

Country name	Population	Capital city	Time in capital (ahead or behind G.M.T.)	Currency
SENEGAL	5,114,600	Dakar	G.M.T.	African financial community franc
SEYCHELLES	59,226	Victoria	4 hours ahead	Seychelles rupee (100 cents)
SIERRA LEONE	3,111,000	Freetown	G.M.T.	Leone (100 cents)
SINGAPORE	2,278,200	Singapore	7½ hours ahead	Singaporean dollar (100 cents)
SOLOMON ISLANDS	250,000	Honiara	11½ hours ahead	Australian dollar
SOMALIA	3,261,000	Mogadishu	3 hours ahead	Somali shilling (100 centésimi)
SOUTH AFRICA	26,129,000	Pretoria/Cape Town	2 hours ahead	Rand (100 cents)
SPAIN	35,971,000	Madrid	1 hour ahead	Peseta (100 céntimos)
SRI LANKA	14,270,000	Colombo	5½ hours ahead	Sri Lankan rupee (100 cents)
SUDAN	16,126,000	Khartoum	2 hours ahead	Sudanese pound (100 piastres)
SURINAM	435,000	Paramaribo	3½ hours behind	Surinamese gulden (100 cents)
SWAZILAND	496,835	Mbabane	2 hours ahead	South African rand
SWEDEN	8,222,310	Stockholm	1 hour ahead	Swedish krona (100 öre)
SWITZERLAND	6,431,000	Berne	1 hour ahead	Swiss franc (100 rappen/centimes)
SYRIA	7,595,895	Damascus	2 hours ahead	Syrian pound (100 piastres)
TAIWAN	16,092,160	Taipei	8 hours ahead	New Taiwan dollar (100 cents)
TANZANIA	15,606,923	Dar es Salaam	3 hours ahead	Tanzanian shilling (100 cents)
THAILAND	42,960,000	Bangkok	7 hours ahead	Baht (100 satangs)
TOGO	2,283,350	Lomé	G.M.T.	African financial community franc
TONGA	94,000	Nuku'alofa	13 hours ahead	Pa'anga (100 seniti)
TRINIDAD AND TOBAGO	1,081,550	Port-of-Spain	5 hours behind	Trinidad and Tobago dollar (100 cents)
TUNISIA	5,737,000	Tunis	1 hour ahead	Tunisian dinar (100 millimes)
TURKEY	40,163,400	Ankara	2 hours ahead	Turkish lira (100 kurus)
UGANDA	11,942,690	Kampala	3 hours ahead	Ugandan shilling (100 cents)
UNION OF SOVIET SOCIALIST REPUBLICS	256,670,000	Moscow	3 hours ahead	Rouble (100 kopeks)
UNITED ARAB EMIRATES	229,000	Abu Dhabi	4 hours ahead	United Arab Emirates dirham (100 fils)
UNITED KINGDOM	54,425,000	London	G.M.T.	Sterling pound (100 pence)
UNITED STATES OF AMERICA	212,300,000	Washington D.C.	5 hours behind	U.S. dollar (100 cents)
UPPER VOLTA	6,174,000	Ouagadougou	G.M.T.	African financial community franc
URUGUAY	3,101,000	Montevideo	3 hours behind	New Uruguayan peso (100 centesimos)
VATICAN CITY	722	Vatican City	1 hour ahead	Italian lira
VENEZUELA	12,361,090	Caracas	4 hours behind	Bolivar (100 céntimos)
VIETNAM	43,741,375	Hanoi	7 hours ahead	Dông (100 xu)
WESTERN SAMOA	159,000	Apia	11 hours behind	Tala (100 sene)
NORTH YEMEN	6,870,000	Sana'a	3 hours ahead	Yemeni riyal (100 fils)
SOUTH YEMEN	1,657,000	Aden	3 hours ahead	Yemeni dinar (1000 fils)
YUGOSLAVIA	21,560,000	Belgrade	1 hour ahead	Yugoslavian dinar (100 para)
ZAIRE	25,629,237	Kinshasa	1 hour ahead	Zaire (100 makuta)
ZAMBIA	5,182,000	Lusaka	2 hours ahead	Zambian kwacha (100 ngwee)

Index

Countries and their capital cities, populations, currencies and local times are listed in the chart on pages 28-31 and are not indexed here.

The information in this book is based on statistics from the following:
United Nations Statistical Yearbook 1976
United Nations Demographic Yearbooks 1975 and 1976
United Nations Yearbook of Industrial Statistics 1976
FAO Production Yearbook 1976
FAO Yearbook of Forest Products 1976
United Nations Compendium of Housing Statistics 1972-1974
The Economist: The World in Figures 1976
B.P. Statistical Review of the World Oil Industry 1976
UNESCO Statistical Yearbook 1976
Statistics of Hunger: Freedom from Hunger Campaign Publication
Civil Aviation Authority
London Weather Centre
Wine and Spirit Association of Great Britain
Joint Statistics Committee of the Chocolate and Sugar Confectionery Industries
U.S. Bureau of Mines Statistics

Pen-friends

If you would like a pen-friend in another country, you can write to one of these addresses, sending details of your age and hobbies and name and address. You should also send a stamped envelope with your name and address on it for them to send their reply.

If you live in Britain you can write to: Central Bureau for Educational Visits and Exchanges, 43 Dorset Street, London, W13 HFN.

If you live in Australia or New Zealand you can write to: Mrs G. Hibberd, International Correspondence for Schools, U.N.A.A., G.P.O. Box 1547, Sydney, N.S.W. 2001, Australia.

If you live in Canada you can write to: Mme Asselin, Bureau de C.S.I. Quebec, Haut Commissariat à la Jeunesse aux Loisirs et aux Sports, Edifice G, 7ème Etage, 1035, Rue de la Chevrotière, Quebec.